T0339850

KURDISTAN:

Achievable reality,
or political mirage?

Mariam Jooma Çarıkçı

AMEC

AMEC

Published by the Afro-Middle East Centre
PO Box 411494, Craighall, 2024, South Africa
www.amec.org.za

First published 2013

ISBN (soft cover) 978-0-9921998-4-5

Copyedited by Tessa Botha, Na'eem Jeenah
Cover Design, Designed and Typeset by Afro-Middle East Centre
Printed by Impress Printers

Contents

List of figures

Frequently used abbreviations and acronyms

AKP – Adalet ve Kalkinma Partisi (Justice and Development Party)

BDP – Baris ve Demokrasi Partisi (Peace and Democracy Party)

CHP – Cumhuriyetci Halk Partisi (Republican People's Party)

GAP – Güneydoğu Anadolu Projesi (Southeastern Anatolia Project)

KCK – Koma Ciwaken Kurdistan (Union of Communities in Kurdistan)

KDP – Partiya Demokrata Kurdistan (Kurdistan Democratic Party)

KNC – Kurdistan National Council

KRG – Hikumeti Heremi Kurdistan (Kurdistan Regional Government)

LCC – Local Coordination Committees, Syria

MHP – Milliyetci Hareket Partisi (Nationalist Action Party)

PJAK – Partiya Jiyana Azad a Kurdistane (Party of Free Life of Kurdistan)

PKK – Partiya Karkeren Kurdistan (Kurdistan Workers' Party)

PUK – Yeketi Nistimani Kurdistan (Patriotic Union of Kurdistan)

PYD – Partiya Yekitia Demokrat (Democratic Union Party)

SNC – Syrian National Council

Acknowledgements

Writing on a topic as vast and complex as that regarding the Kurds of the Middle East requires more than just a sound background on the political and social history of the region. I am indebted to my husband, Refik, for having guided me to areas of research and to sources that I would otherwise not have accessed. I also greatly appreciate his generosity in taking on a double burden of babysitting, to allow me to complete this work.

I am hopeful that this book will provide a broad, yet substantive, background read for anyone with an interest in the region.

Introduction

Kurdistan has historically been regarded as a geocultural region where four volatile Middle East states – Turkey, Iraq, Syria and Iran – converge. For the estimated twenty to thirty million Kurds spread across these four countries, the idea of a separate and independent homeland has, over recent decades become a political goal. Kurdish movements, both military and political, have cited the legal discrimination against Kurdish political parties, their limited representation in the cultural and social life of the countries they reside in, and restrictions on the use of Kurdish languages as major reasons for the call to separatism. Certainly, one could say that a sense of 'Kurdishness' has grown considerably as a result of globalisation and social media, creating a more ethnocentric understanding of what it means to be part of an international Kurdish community. In the current Middle Eastern context, the aspirations of the Kurdish people have become intimately linked to the question of broader democratic transformation in the region.

As the war in Syria continues unabated, Syrian Kurds face a familiar dilemma, either to be used as a proxy force by the regime of Bashar al-Asad or to join the embattled opposition camp that may represent a diversity of views on the shape of a postAsad state. Indeed, the developments in Syria could not have come at a more inopportune time for Turkey as it begins its nascent journey towards a peace agreement with its own Kurds, and embarks on a process of constitutional reform. Iraq, too, is heavily embroiled in contestation

1

between its northern autonomous Kurdish region and the south of the country. It is clear that the impasse regarding the Kurdish population in the Middle East is no longer sustainable. This book explores the relations between the Kurdish movements and the states of Turkey, Iraq, Syria and Iran, with a view to highlighting the historical background and major challenges facing the idea of the creation of a separate Kurdish state.

Geographically, Kurdistan is a heavily mountainous region, a factor that has both helped and hindered Kurdish unity. While the geography has benefited the Kurdish movements in terms of providing a safe haven for armed groups, it has also been a considerable factor in the chronic disunity of the broader Kurdish population, as factions tend to be split between the Kurdish Workers Party's (PKK) headquarters in the Kandil Mountain range and those that operate within the four countries themselves. While semi-independent Kurdish emirates such as Ardalan existed into the middle of the nineteenth century, there has never been an independent Kurdistan in the sense of a modern state.[1] The dramatic changes in technology over the past decade have, however, facilitated the creation of a 'cyber Kurdistan', which has been shaped and influenced, in particular, by Kurdish youth in the diaspora.

The modern Republic of Turkey was created in 1923, after the fall of the Ottoman Empire, which was established in 1299. Its collapse was followed by the colonial division of the Middle East and the creation of Turkey. Since then, challenges regarding inclusive citizenship and pluralism in the region have remained markedly unresolved. As home to the largest number of Kurds, Turkey's approach to the Kurdish question has, consequently, defined regional Kurdish politics. Certainly, the virulently secular and nationalist Turkish state policy under Kemal Ataturk's influence has been a major cause for the creation of a secular-religious binary that remains at the heart of Turkish politic, impacting on how any efforts

2

to address Kurdish grievances are shaped. Modern Turkey's historical alliances with countries such as Israel, as well as the USA, have created a palpable sense of its ideological alienation from the rest of the region. Syria, Iraq and Iran have, in turn, treated their own Kurdish citizens as foreign policy tools that can be used to appease or antagonise their neighbours, whom they have been loath to trust.

In Iraq, Saddam Hussein's regime attempted to physically annihilate Iraqi Kurds using various methods of mass murder, despite their legal status as a recognised minority. More recently, Kurds have increasingly played an influential role in determining the course of political action in the region, to the extent that in Iraq they have been described as the 'kingmakers of Baghdad'. This shift is largely due to the 2003 US invasion of Iraq and raises important questions about whether a precedent may have been set for Kurds in surrounding states who may have to cede territory for the creation of further Kurdish enclaves.

Taking advantage of the ongoing cleavages in state power across the region, the Kurdish movements have greater visibility in Syria and Iraq, a factor that will undoubtedly impact on Turkey's domestic Kurdish issue. The question of whether a state of 'Kurdistan' might indeed be the solution to a conflict that has claimed tens of thousands of lives – 40 000 1984 in Turkey alone – is being debated again.

Chronic fragmentation among Kurdish groups that have often sought to secure their own interests at the expense of sister movements in other countries has, however, complicated matters further. As Fred Halliday[2] suggests in his analysis of the myriad armed groups, 'Kurdish nationalist movements have sought support and established ad hoc alliances with neighbouring states, even if this has meant neglecting or betraying the oppressed Kurds within those very same states.' The fracturing of Kurdish groups therefore calls into question the hegemony of a single Kurdish discourse. In the absence of a viable contiguous geographical region that could be demarcated as majority Kurdish (aside from northern Iraq) and a unified Kurdish voice, attempts at creating a state of Kurdistan raise more questions than may be resolved.

Differences in the status of Kurdish groups across the region further underscore the complexity of the political landscape and the unlikely creation of a 'united' Kurdistan inclusive of all Kurds from the four countries. From the armed and highly organised Kurdish Workers' Party (PKK) – considered a terrorist group by Turkey, the USA, the European Union and the UN – to the fledgling Kurdish-administered areas of conflict-stricken Syria and the internationally recognised and supported Kurdistan Autonomous Government (KRG) in northern Iraq, Kurds of the region are confronted with competing challenges that make all attempts at peace a crucial regional issue.

Moreover, overarching concerns regarding democratic pluralism, including, but not limited to, Kurdish populations in the region as a whole, highlight the need for deeper institutional changes within these states. It has been suggested that the creation of a Kurdistan state in such a context would be the equivalent of using a small adhesive bandage to heal a gaping bullet wound.

This book argues that, despite the increasing popularity of Kurdish nationalism across the region, the foundation of a Kurdish state based on 'ethnicity' as a defining feature of its citizenry runs contrary to the democratic transformation that minority groups and civil society actors in the region have long been agitating for. Indeed, it would reassert the false basis of ethnicity as a foundation for the nation state at a time when identity politics has been a major cause for instability across Syria, Iraq, Iran and Turkey.

The historical relations between each of these four states and their Kurdish populations will be examined, beginning with an overview of the Kurds as a nation across these states. This is followed by an explanation of the shift in regional power relations caused by the collapse of the Ottoman Empire, and the creation of modern

Turkey, as well as the spectacular rise of the Justice and Development Party (AKP) in 2002. Chapter Three looks at the formation of the Kurdish Workers' Party (PKK), the primary Kurdish armed opposition group in Turkey, with a view to understanding the prospects for its future in the context of current developments in Turkish politics. Chapter Four focuses on the changing fortunes of Iraqi Kurds and their dramatic rise to power following the US invasion of Iraq in 2003. It argues that, despite Iraqi Kurdistan's economic success, the road to fully-fledged independence still depends on the political climate of the region. It argues that the cohesion of Kurdish movements is a critical factor in either facilitating or sabotaging Kurdish aspirations in Iraq. Moreover, there is a critical need for an improvement in relations between Erbil, the capital of Northern Iraq, and Baghdad, without which democratic and inclusive politics is likely to elude Iraq. Erbil's autonomous administration is still dependent on power sharing of energy revenues with Baghdad which has become an extremely contentious issue as the KRG has signed exploration contracts with large oil concerns without Baghdad's approval.

Syria's Kurds are the focus of Chapter Five, and the relations between the Syrian regime, opposition groups and Kurdish movements are explored in some detail. The nuanced differences that exist between the Kurdish Syrian youth and the established political Kurdish parties are also discussed. Finally, Chapter Six offers an overview of Iranian Kurds as a political entity, and argues that the theocratic state's monopoly of power and its historical sponsorship of Kurdish movements elsewhere have silenced domestic Kurdish voices.

Chapter One
Who are the Kurds?

The Kurds are believed to be descendants of Indo-European people who inhabited the mountainous regions between Iraq, Turkey, Iran and Syria. While most Kurds profess to be Sunni Muslims, a smaller number are Shi'a Muslims, followed by adherents of the Alevi sect of Shi'a Islam. It is, however, difficult precisely to determine what the distribution of faith allegiances is.

The Kurdish language is not homogenous, and is generally divided into its main variants – Kurmanci, Sorani and Zazaki – each with various dialects. In practice, each of these languages is distinct from the others, with few overlapping commonalities. This added another obstacle to cohesion amongst the various Kurdish groups.[1]

During Ottoman rule, Kurds lived a nomadic lifestyle dictated by the seasons, and constantly migrated across their shared territory. This relationship to the land was dramatically altered in the aftermath of the First World War, with the signing of the Treaty of Sevres in 1920 and the imposition of the infamous Sykes-Picot Agreement. (See Figure 1 for map of Sykes-Picot division.) These treaties determined the borders that created the new states of Iraq, Syria and Kuwait in the interests of the prevailing imperial powers. The Sevres Treaty included the possibility of creating a new Kurdish state, but this was never implemented. The Turkish War of Independence ended with the ousting of the occupying forces, the abolition of the Ottoman Caliphate and the creation of the Republic of

Turkey in 1923.

Modern Turkey was then led by military commander Kemal Ataturk, whose secular nationalist ideology (termed 'Kemalism') became and remains a major defining force in modern Turkish politics. The Kemalist state was based on the denial and exclusion of Islam from public life, and regulated the practice of religion in the private sphere of Turkish life. Citizenship was defined through the prism of 'Turkishness' or Turk Milleti (this has now changed to Turkiye Milleti, roughly translated as 'citizen of Turkey' rather than 'Turkish citizen'). Secularism and westernisation were seen as the keys to creating a modern state, and anything that suggested a connection to 'Arab Islam' was violently suppressed. It has been argued that by politicising ethnicity, Kemalism created both an insoluble problem that condemned the Turkish state to endless conflict with its own population, as well as chronic tensions with its neighbours.[2]

Today, Turkey's Kurdish population is estimated at between fifteen and twenty per cent of its eighty million population. Opposition to the centralist Turkish regime began with rebellions as early as 1925, inspired by a mixture of Islamist and Kurdish nationalist sentiment. Intermittent waves of protest were then reshaped in the early 1980s under a Marxist ideological umbrella, and through the founding of the armed PKK. This was at a time when Turkey was a strong ally of anticommunist superpower, the USA. The Turkish state is currently at a crossroads in its historical battle with the PKK after the reopening of talks with the group, a development that is impacting on it relations with its Kurdish citizenry in general.

Kurds in Iraq account for between fifteen and twenty per cent of the country's population. Iraq's Kurds had also faced repression during the British mandate. Successive Kurdish rebellions were crushed, a situation that did not improve significantly under the Iraqi Ba'athist regime, despite legal rights to the use of mother tongue

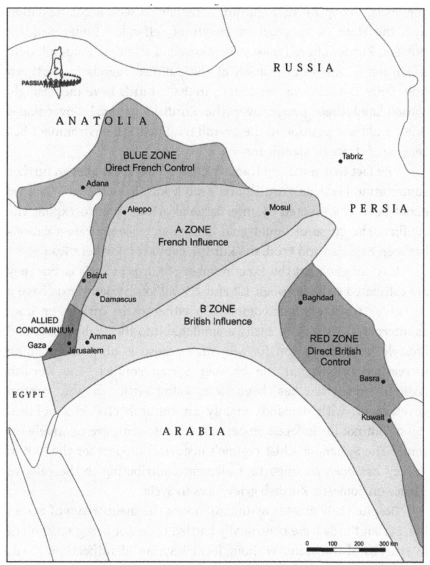

Figure 1: Sykes-Picot Agreement, 1916.[3]

languages and limited self-rule granted under the first Iraqi Constitution of 1958. The central government was adept at coopting its Kurdish population, leading to a confusing set of strategic dilemmas among Kurds regarding whether to seek accommodation with the state or to rebel in favour of self-rule.[4] Under Saddam Hussein, Kurds suffered mass executions and attempted annihilation, which led to the securitisation of the political agenda in northern Iraq. Since the US invasion of Iraq in 2003, Kurds have increasingly consolidated their power over the Kurdish Regional Government (KRG) and their position in the overall Iraqi political environment has become of strategic significance.

The fact that northern Iraq is rich in oil has created even further contestation between Kurdish and Arab Iraqis, a conflict that has no doubt been exacerbated by international actors keen to exploit the conflict. The curse of liquid gold continues to complicate relations between Baghdad and Erbil, the Kurdish capital of northern Iraq.

It is unclear what the exact number of Kurds in Syria is, but they are estimated to be between 1.7 and 2.5 million. Syrian Kurds have a particular trajectory not common to either their Turkish or Iraqi counterparts. They more easily assimilated into the Arab culture and lifestyle, a likely reason for why their cause is only now gaining increasing visibility in the broader Syrian conflict. The Kurdish position in Syria 'has been less antagonistic to the central government, with demands mainly on cultural, civil and political rights, but not for independence; calls for autonomy are relatively re-cent.'[5] The Syrian Ba'athist regime's historical support for the PKK in Turkey has been an important element contributing to the relative silence on domestic Kurdish grievances in Syria.

Despite their greater assimilation into the mainstream of Syrian life, Syrian Kurds have continually battled their not being recognised as citizens of the state. Without formal Syrian identification, Kurds have been prevented from owning property, participating in elections or benefiting from food subsidies.[6] The ongoing two-year-old conflict in Syria has reconfigured power relations between various Syrian Kurdish groups and the Arab Syrian opposition to Bashar al-Asad's

Figure 2: Kurdish-inhabited area in Turkey, Iraq, Syria and Iran

regime. The withdrawal of Asad's forces from northern Syria has allowed the main Kurdish armed group, the Democratic Union Party (PYD), to take control of the area, raising hopes of greater visibility of Kurdish grievances. However, the dependency of Syrian Kurds on their Turkish and Iraqi counterparts for material and political support continues to make the creation of a formidable domestic Kurdish opposition in Syria unlikely.

The Kurds of Iran have had limited success in raising their

political aspirations onto the Iranian political agenda. The overlap between Persian culture and the Persian language with Kurdish dialects has contributed to greater assimilation of Kurds in Iran than their counterparts in Turkey. However, the silence on Kurdish rights in Iran is also due to a ruling authoritarian regime that has shown little tolerance for dissidence. Iranian Kurds find themselves in a dual dilemma, being both a minority ethnic group with allegiances to communities across the border, as well as being largely Sunni Muslims in a dominant Shi'a theocratic state.

The Party of Free Life of Kurdistan (PJAK) is currently the most significant Kurdish armed force in Iran. PJAK has, unlike other groups which have confined themselves to cross-border operations, taken to urban warfare within Iran itself. However, Iran's status as a sponsor of Iraqi, Syrian and Turkish Kurds at different times limits PJAK from any substantive political manoeuvring domestically.

Chapter Two
Pseudocitizens in ultranationalist Turkey

The fall of the Ottoman Empire and the dramatic change in the power landscape across the Eurasia in the early twentieth century created a crisis of identity for the new leaders of the Republic of Turkey. No longer were Islamic civilisation and the caliphate seen as a high point of the development of the Ottoman Empire, but were considered to be a contributing factor to the near partition of Anatolia by the French and British during the First World War. Between 1911 and 1913, the Ottoman Empire lost more than one-third of its territory and one-fifth of its population.[1] In order to gain maximum strength for the 1915-1916 military campaign, General Mustafa Kemal, who later assumed the name 'Ataturk' or 'father of the Turks', rallied Muslims under the banner of Islam, an ideology he would discard soon after the formation of the republic. Under the military leadership of Kemal, remnants of the old Ottoman military, and the war-ravaged population, were able to drive out the invasion forces. Victory over the European powers at the Battle of Gallipoli remains a defining moment in the Turkish historical psyche. It has been used to great effect by successive regimes as a propaganda tool to create nationalist unity. Kurds, like many other ethnic minorities from the Caucus region, were part of the forces which drove out the invading forces. However, as the Turkish state solidified its hegemony over the definition of citizenship, state language used to describe Kurdish

Turks also evolved. There was a marked shift between the early years of the republic, when Kurds were considered brothers-in-arms in the fight against foreign powers, to the political discourse of the 1990s, when it changed to a more alienating language that characterised Turkey's Kurds as disloyal pseudocitizens.[2]

In an epic change of destiny, the republic's early state policy no longer aligned itself with its Muslim neighbours, but sought to embrace a materialist philosophy of progress. Mustafa Kemal espoused a form of social engineering that scrapped Shari'ah law, revised the entire Ottoman Turkish language to remove Arabic and Persian vocabulary, adopted the Roman alphabet and, importantly, outlawed religious meetings in both the private and public spheres. Sheikhs and community leaders who engaged in the recital of the Qur'an or in dhikr (remembrance) meetings were imprisoned or hanged. Equally, the use of the Kurdish language was banned, and restrictions were placed on the public practice of Kurdish cultural festivals.

Under this system, the common citizen was not deemed educated enough to direct the revolutionary change to modernise the country, and, instead, had to be led by the ruling elite in the interests of the people as a whole. The nature of those interests was, of course, also defined by the rulers and not the ruled. The transnational nature of Islam, as experienced under Ottoman influence, was a threat to the new state-centred ideology that defined borders, languages and orientation for its people. Thus, the Kurds, Albanians, Bosnians, Circassians, Laz and Pomaks all had to assimilate into the Turkish nation state.

Rebellion by both the Kurds and devout Muslims began early in the republic's history. Their first major armed resistance initiative was joined by Sheikh Said, leader of the Sufi Naqshbandi tarikat (Sufi order), a Kurd himself, who led a revolt against the state, in what has come to be acknowledged as joint opposition by both Kurdish nationalists and Islamists, who were both seen as enemies of the new, secular Turkish nation.

What is of great significance is the sectarian fallout that manifested itself during this rebellion. The Sunni Sheikh was opposed by a faction of Alevi Kurds, who threw in their weight behind the Turkish state against fellow Kurds who were Sunnis. The Kurdish movement has famously been unable to consolidate itself as a homogenous entity, leading to the use of the Kurdish people as proxy forces for opposing aims.

Modern Turkey

The Kurdish question has unquestionably been the defining issue of modern Turkey's domestic and regional politics. The devastating cross border conflict between the Turkish state and the PKK has claimed some 40 000 lives since 1984 in Turkey alone.[3] The Turkish Ministry of Labor has suggested that the country has lost some US$400 billion since the onset of armed hostilities.[4] The figure is contested, but analysts agree that the price of the conflict to the developing economy has been severe.

Since its creation as a republic, the centralist and nationalist policies of the Kemal Ataturk regime have sought to mark Turkey as a homogenous, monolinguistic, secular nation state. This had dire consequences for the social and cultural freedoms of those who are devout Muslims and minorities such as the Kurds. Moreover, the converging interests between the military, who viewed themselves as the protectors of the secular republic, and the Turkish political establishment meant that resistance to Turkish nationalism was bound to transform into an armed struggle. Following the onset of the Cold War, Turkey was seen as a trustworthy western ally, loyal to the western security establishment of the time, which became a significant factor in the preference for stability over democracy by both the Turkish military elite and western allies, and came to define

Turkish politics.

Fast forward to 2013, and Turkey is a markedly different country on the brink of what many expect to be a historic transformation in its relations with its Kurdish population that will have a far-reaching impact on overall personal freedoms in the country. As Reynolds[5] suggested in his analysis of the new regime, 'The old but comforting bromides about Turkey being the staunchly pro-Western creation of Mustafa Kemal Ataturk have long ceased to be reliable guides to Turkish behaviour.'

In a biting opinion piece for the English daily, *Today's Zaman*, Eyten Mahcupyan explained: 'Today the opposite of what the Republican regime imagined has been realised: The religious are ruling the country and offering to grant rights to Kurds.'[6] But, just as this fragile moment between the state and the PKK may come to define a refreshing new way of considering state-society relations in Turkey, analysts and participants remain cautiously optimistic about the outcome as they consider the long history of failed peace processes. In the months preceding the formal initiation of talks between the PKK and the intelligence services in January 2013, an estimated 900 people were killed in armed clashes. Moreover, the PKK is not simply an armed movement; indeed, its involvement in the global narcotics trade and in money laundering has earned it an international terrorist label. Thus the economics of war may prove to be more profitable than stability and peace, raising the stakes for a postconflict scenario.

AKP's meteoric rise and its impact on the PKK

From the outset, developments in Turkey may seem to contradict the trends in Iraq's Kurdish Regional Government (KRG) region or northern Syria where PKK affiliate, the PYD, has gained significant control of territory. However, the shift from a mentality of 'eliminating' the PKK towards engaging the group considered a 'terror organisation' by the UN, among others, is due to a vivid change in both Turkey's regional and international presence, which itself is the result of the adoption of an alternative foreign policy. Some have suggested that this change of direction contains 'echoes of empire' as a throwback to an Ottoman-inspired regional policy.[7] Whether or not that underpins the ideological thrust behind the development of the ruling AK Party's foreign policy is unclear. What is lucid, however, is that rather than pursuing a failing military campaign against the PKK, the ruling party is now engaging in inclusive politics, which they believe may save the country from both the kind of ethnic separatism that threatens Iraq and Syria, and will ensure greater freedoms for the majority of Turkey's Muslim population, its primary support base.

The AKP's rise to power has been nothing short of spectacular, considering the environment from which it had emerged. In the June 2011 elections, the party took some fifty per cent of the national vote, which included parts of Kurdish-dominated areas. Participation in the elections was eighty-seven per cent and the representivity of parliament increased to ninety-five per cent.[8] These statistics reflect two major trends in Turkish sociopolitics. The first was a sense of weariness with the old Kemalist world view that had been unable to produce dynamic solutions to the multiplicity of issues affecting Turkey. Second was the rise of a new wealthy middle class which, unlike its parents' generation, is university educated yet identifies with the traditional values espoused by the AKP.

Turkey has also markedly increased its regional presence by mediating or becoming involved in the politics of its neighbours. An apt example is the downgrading of its diplomatic relations with Israel which, under the Republican People's Party (CHP), was considered a strong ally of the state in a hostile 'reactionary' neighbourhood. Prime Minister Recep Tayyip Erdoğan's bold critiques of Zionism, and Turkey's aid to the Palestinian people have not harmed his status among citizens of surrounding conflict-torn Arab states. It is certainly a marked change from the attempts by the previous establishment to 'Turkify Islam' and project an image of being definitively 'non-Arab'. Moreover, Israel's recent apology to Turkey regarding the controversial killing of nine activists on the humanitarian flotilla destined for Gaza signals recognition from both the USA and Israel of Turkey's strengthening regional position. Turkey's increasing economic, and to an extent political, relationship with Iran, particularly over the question of the latter's nuclear development programme, has given it more leverage in its diplomatic role in the region as a whole. Greater economic growth and wealth have been instrumental to newfound Turkish confidence in its trade relations with the 'East', a change best exemplified in its robust trade relations with the KRG.

Ironically, it was the Islamist AK Party that used the benchmarks needed for European Union membership as a means to introduce democratic reforms. This has, in effect, caused much debate in Turkey about the 'meaning of democracy', as Kemalists distance themselves from a concept of democracy that includes religious freedoms such as the wearing of headscarves by government employees. Berna Turam highlighted some of the feelings of those who oppose the AK Party's rule. One Kemalist told her: 'The West and the EU do not understand the sacred meaning of the military for the Turkish society. In our country, there is no difference between an NGO and the military, each of which come to rescue us from political or natural disasters such as Sharia or Earthquake.'[9]

Michael Reynolds[10] encapsulated the contradiction that the new ruling class created for observers attempting to make sense of Turkish politics. He explains:

> However important this broader question of Islam and
> democracy may be, it has led analysts of Turkish politics

to ask the wrong question of whether Turkey's new
leaders are understood best as liberal democrats or as
Muslims...What analysts operating within this
framework miss is that the question is largely irrelevant
to understanding Turkish foreign policy. In formulating
their policies, the AKP's leaders do not see a dichotomy
between Islam and democracy.

The change in Turkey's political landscape has upset members of
the old guard, especially those who have benefited materially and
politically from the military-judicial nexus over the three decades of
conflict. In 2009, Turkey began what the state called 'democratic
opening', to engage with the PKK through the disarmament of the
fighters of the Kurdish group. The state reviewed this approach after
an incident in 2009 when amnesty was given to a group of eight
fighters who crossed into Turkey from Iraq at the Habur border gate,
and whose return was then jubilantly celebrated by many Kurds in
the country. Kurds regarded the return of their fighters as a victory
over the Turkish state, and this resulted in a nationalist backlash in
western Turkey. Fears of an outbreak of major violence led to the
cancellation of further amnesty of PKK fighters.

Following this, Erdoğan and the AKP changed their focus to
increasing civilian oversight of the military, which has led to a
marked taming of the army from its former status as default guardian
of the Republic. This change has allowed greater civilian ownership
over the political process in the country, but has not been able to
fully convince the staunchly nationalist political parties of the need
for a new problem-solving paradigm.

The main opposition parties – the CHP and the Nationalist
Movement Party (MHP) – continue to conduct politics on a basis
where they oppose any proposals by the AKP, an approach that is not
always constructive and yields not substantive contribution from the

opposition. One example of this would be a CHP delegation's visit to Syria in March 2013, which included talks with Bashar al-Asad aimed at distancing Turkey from involvement in the conflict. News reports quoted the delegation as stressing 'the Turkish people's refusal to interfere in Syrian affairs, and its commitment to good neighbourly relations'.[11] The CHP is seeking to make itself relevant in a rapidly changing environment unsuited to its centralist and nationalist ideology. In such a climate of few alternatives, the Kurdish movements themselves have acknowledged that the current process may be the first substantial political attempt to end the conflict.

It is evident that the peace process will alter the environment for both the ruling and opposition parties in Turkey, causing the latter to reconsider how relevant they may be in Turkey in the current political climate. More importantly it will raise questions of how the PKK and the pro-Kurdish Peace and Democracy Party (BDP) might transform themselves from single-issue organisations into participants in a fragile multi-party system. In the context of the Gezi park protests which began on 28 May and resulted in severe critiques of Erdoğan's leadership style by disaffected groups, the ruling AKP will have to tread very carefully amongst the new actors, who will no doubt accept nothing less than full participation in Turkey's destiny. This is particularly so since the AKP is preparing for elections scheduled for 2014.

Chapter Three
The future of the PKK

Abdullah Öcalan established the Kurdish Workers' Party (PKK) in 1978 against the backdrop of the Cold War and Turkey's status as a staunch ally of the western superpowers. It was a product of the leftist Turkish movements of the 1960s and 1970s, and was, arguably, more ideologically nuanced than its current status as promoter of Kurdish nationalism might suggest. Öcalan founded his party on the precepts of Marxist-Leninism, and it consequently came to be regarded as a 'communist enemy' by the US-supported Turkish state.

The PKK gained prominence not only for its organisational tactics against the Turkish state, but also for its ability to influence regional Kurdish politics. It finds itself in the unusual position of being an armed and internationally denounced terrorist organisation that is the key partner with which the Turkish state is engaging. A superficial analysis of the historical problems in Turkey may suggest that, rather than engaging the PKK, the government should seek to work with legal political structures that represent Kurdish interests, such as the BDP. While such an analysis might make sense in another context, in Turkey the PKK stands out as being far more influential than the BDP, which is essentially subservient to the commands of the umbrella organisation, the Union of Communities in Kurdistan (KCK), and the KCK is, in turn, directly influenced by Öcalan. This is evidenced by the fact that Kurds have, since 2002, voted for non-traditional Kurdish parties during elections, yet still view the PKK as

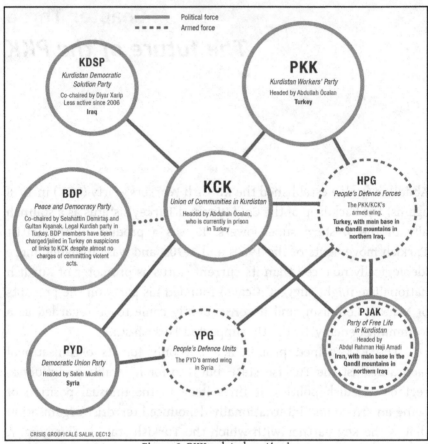

Figure 3: PKK-related parties.[1]

the guardian of the Kurdish cause. These attitudes suggest that the Kurdish question is inseparable from the PKK, mainly because Öcalan represents the 'unrivaled single authority of the organisation'.[2] He thus plays a crucial leadership role in influencing the cessation or continuation of violence.

It was perhaps Öcalan's capture in 1999, and his subsequent imprisonment on Imrali Island (a narrow escape from the death penalty to which he had originally been sentenced) that reinforced his cult status. Since then, he has become the PKK's final authority on everything to do with the Kurdish question and the armed struggle. Moreover, the KCK, created in 2007 with Öcalan as its honorary leader, has solidified the relevance of the PKK to regional politics since its membership includes PJAK (from Iran), PYD (from Syria) and smaller Iraqi Kurdish parties.

This is not to suggest that the PKK's leadership is uncontested. There have certainly been undercurrents of disagreement between different levels of and personalities in authority, particularly between Kurdish nationalists in Erbil and those loyal to Öcalan. Murat Karayilan, Öcalan's deputy and the acting leader of the PKK since Öcalan's detention, is often portrayed by the media as a possible rival to the imprisoned leader. However, the PKK is not known for its acceptance of dissension within its ranks and has created a strong top-down organisational structure. Dissidents are often brutally dealt with. Öcalan's role as chief mediator between the government and the PKK is a test of whether he is indeed the supreme leader of the organisation, capable of reining in factions that may want to derail the process.

While the PKK's link to the general Kurdish population of Turkey may be a bitter pill to swallow for military and intelligence officers who have battled the organisation in the field, Öcalan also represents an ageing Kurdish generation that may be better disposed to accommodation with Turkey. This is in contrast to the vastly more radical Kurdish youth who have developed a greater sense of 'Kurdishness' and who bear the greatest burden of the bad economic policies of successive Turkish regimes which led to the country's underdevelopment. Should the peace process fail, these youth would be a significant force in the renewal of all-out conflict.

Imrali talks: High stakes

It was a tense and fragile time for Turkey as a nascent peace process began in earnest early this January. Two representatives of the

Kurdish BDP and the head of Turkey's National Intelligence Organization (MIT) met with Abdullah Öcalan on Imrali Island on 4 January. The meeting was touted as the start of a new era, with subsequent visits suggesting the possibility of political negotiations and an eventual peace accord between the state and the PKK. However, just days after the first meeting, three PKK activists – one of whom was a confidant of Öcalan – were killed in Paris. State security agencies were on high alert during the funeral services of the three women, as a slide back to hostilities could easily have occurred. However, the mass funerals proceeded peacefully, with both sides preferring to remain silent on who may have been responsible for the crimes. Indeed, one placard at the Diyarbakir memorial service aptly encapsulated the war weariness on both sides of the conflict, proclaiming: 'No winners in war, No losers in peace'.

The talks between the PKK and the state are reportedly focused on four main proposals. The first and most crucial at this stage is a commitment to halt hostilities. Öcalan signalled the beginning of a complete ceasefire on 21 March 2013, the official start of the Kurdish New year (Navruz) festival. His speech was read out at a rally in the Kurdish stronghold city of Diyarbakir, where thousands of Kurds converged for the Navruz celebrations. This was a major step in the beginning of a sustainable peace process. Öcalan told the gathering, 'The stage has been reached where our armed forces should withdraw beyond the borders...It's not the end. It's the start of a new era.'[3]

Secondly, a new judicial reform package is envisaged, one in which the Counter Terrorism Law would be changed so that 'incitement of violence' must be established by the prosecutor in order to pursue suspects charged with promoting propaganda on behalf of terrorist organisations. A change to this law could impact upon hundreds of members and intellectuals of the KCK's urban wing who were arrested under existing legislation. The third proposal lies at the heart of a reconfiguration of the definition of 'citizenship' and will require constitutional reformation to embrace a neutral wording of what it means to be a citizen of Turkey. Finally, the freedom to be taught in Kurdish mother tongue at schools has been an important demand of the Kurdish movements, which see the barriers to such education as contradictory to the spirit of an inclusive Turkish state.

In addition to these four main proposals, there will also undoubtedly be discussions on lowering the national election threshold from ten per cent to the European norm of five per cent, to allow the BDP a fair chance at the polls. Needless to say, with such broad reforms on the agenda, there will certainly be a revision of the centralist model of governance to ensure better administration in formerly underdeveloped areas.

There has, thus far, been goodwill from both sides on aspects of the main proposals. The PKK, for its part, released eight government workers it had kidnapped on various occasions. The exchange, which took place after Öcalan called for the release, was far removed from the atmosphere in Habur in 2009 when amnesty was given to thirty-four PKK members to return to Turkey. The Habur incident quickly turned sour when the PKK group was received in a defiant and triumphant spirit by its supporters, resulting in unhappiness from Turkish nationalists over the deaths of Turkish soldiers killed by the PKK. Under the conditions of the latest peace initiative, plans to disarm and demobilise on Turkish soil began to take effect on 8 May 2013 after a public announcement by the PKK.

The Counter Terrorism Bill, which will require the agreement of all Turkey's main political parties, has been submitted for Parliament's approval. This highlights the fact that, despite its electoral hegemony, the AKP does not have the absolute majority needed to make any unilateral changes to the constitution. It is still dependent on compromise to push forth its envisaged reforms, which include the adoption of a new constitution. The current constitution is a remnant of the 1982 military coup and faces a 'serious legitimacy problem'.[4] The AKP used the promise of constitutional reform as a key part of its 2011 election campaign, and the pressure is now on for it to find ways to make it a reality.

A Constitution Consensus Committee, composed of three representatives from each of the four main parties, has been tasked with overseeing the process of constitutional reform. It began a series of meetings in October 2012. Two key elements of the committee's rules and procedures are the need for consultation with the Turkish public and total consensus from all parties before adopting any decisions.

Strikingly absent from the discussions between the PKK and the government is the demand for territorial independence or regional autonomy. Some analysts have suggested that the PKK has deliberately sidestepped the issue, which may be raised again after the normalisation of relations. The fact that Öcalan called for a withdrawal from Turkey, but not for the laying down of weapons, gives some credence to this view. However, there is resounding consensus on the territorial unity of the country by all the main actors. Nevertheless, there remains nervousness about whether or not the peace process will be used as a means to further a separatist agenda. In such a tense environment, symbols can play a significant role in how both the government and the PKK's actions are judged. For example, the lack of Turkish national flags at the Navruz celebrations was commented on by the major political parties. Turkish president, Abdullah Gül, argued, 'The flag is something for which we even sacrifice our lives when necessary. So, I never think that any of my Kurdish citizens are against this flag. [The absence of Turkish flags in Diyarbakir] is a big mistake and a shortcoming.'[5]

There are critical voices, such as those of Emre Uslu, the USA-based Turkish journalist and former graduate of the police academy, who maintains that the PKK may use this time to widen its sphere of influence, including into northern Syria. According to this view, the decentralisation of local government envisaged through the proposed constitutional reform will only strengthen cross border links between Syrian and Turkish Kurds. Uslu goes so far as to say,

'In other words, because their visions overlap, the PKK and Prime Minister Recep Tayyip Erdoğan will act together in the months to come; it is assumed that regardless of the regime type in Syria, Turkey will have influence from the Turkish border to Aleppo.'[6]

However, it seems analysts are more inclined to believe that the question of secession is no longer on the table for Turkey's PKK and that this development may be attributed to the complex reality of Kurds living across Turkey in their multigenerational diversity. One example of this complexity is that the demarcation of 'Kurdish' areas is not as clear in Turkey as it is in Iraq. The movement of Kurds over decades from Eastern Turkey into the interior of the country has made Istanbul, Antalya and Izmir among the largest demographically Kurdish cities in Turkey. This is a significant factor when we consider the challenges regarding how reforms on decentralisation and language may be implemented.

Chapter Four
Autonomy in post-invasion Iraq

Of the four states most relevant to the Kurdish question, Iraq has most strongly demonstrated the rise of Kurdish power on a state level. Certainly, the internationally-recognised Kurdish Regional Government (KRG), formed with significant US support following its 2003 invasion of Iraq, has given the Kurds of the region renewed inspiration for their cause. The region has transformed itself from being marked with the tragedies of Saddam's extermination campaigns to a powerful economic hub experiencing higher growth rates, stability and foreign investment compared to southern Iraq, which is crippled by the sectarian Sunni-Shi'a divide. From afar, this development may suggest the possibility of fully-fledged independence for Kurdish Iraq. However, internal power struggles directly influenced by patronage from neighbouring states – particularly Iran and Turkey, both of which favour a unified Iraq – remain a major obstacle to substantive independence.

In a remarkable change of historical course, Kurds in Iraq have today gained prominent positions in both the running of the KRG and in the Iraqi federal government. Legislation has ensured that the Kurdish regions have the power to veto or approve any amendments to the Iraqi constitution. Hiltermann suggested that 'because so much of Iraq's parliamentary politics since 2005 has concerned constitutionally mandated legislation, the Kurds have left their imprint repeatedly and decisively.'[1] Today, the positions of president

Figure 4: Kurdish areas in Iraq.

of the republic and leader of the KRG, as well as key positions in the foreign ministry and intelligence services, are held by Kurds.

How did Iraqi Kurds Iraq achieve such a feat, considering the bitter history between the state and its Kurdish population? How will the KRG's experience inform aspiring Kurdish movements in the region? And to what extent can the KRG sustain itself economically and politically as an independent entity, without the patronage of regional players? Furthermore, how can short-term gains and long-term goals be reconciled? It has been argued by analysts like Hiltermann,[2] who view the tension between the Kurds conflicting aims of whether to fight for secession or for greater minority rights, as a leitmotif of their history. In order to answer these questions we need to go back into history and examine the particular relationship that Iraqi Kurds have had with the state since its creation after the Sykes-Picot Agreement.

The Sykes-Picot Agreement was a secret treaty between Britain and France, with the support of Russia, signed in 1916. The imperial powers carved spheres of influence for themselves in anticipation of the fall of the Ottoman Empire after the First World War. According to the agreement, 'Kurdistan' – or the former Ottoman 'Vilayet' areas of Mosul, Baghdad and Basra – would fall under the Russian sphere of influence. In order to secure this territory, the Russians needed both Kurdish and Armenian support in exchange for promises of freedom from Ottoman rule. Motivated by these aims of securing self-government, the Kurds and Armenians took up arms in support of the allies against the Ottoman forces.

However, Russia itself underwent a major change in political and ideological positioning in 1917, as the Bolsheviks, led by Lenin, overthrew the Russian tsar and all remnants of the Russian monarchy. Consistent with their opposition to the monarchy, the Bolsheviks rejected treaties signed by their predecessor governments. Consequently, the Kurds lost both their Russian patrons and the support of Mustafa Kemal, the new leader of the Turkish republic. Kemal used the Kurds to great advantage by rallying them behind the banner of Islam to fight the Allies on Turkey's western flank. However, soon after the establishment of the republic, which had at its heart the values of uncompromising secularism and nationalism, both the Kurds and devout Muslims of Turkey came to be regarded as enemies of the state.

This contextual history is important to consider, particularly when trying to locate current Kurdish leadership struggles. The British quickly filled the gap left by the Russians, and ruled Iraq as a mandate from the League of Nations. It was under British administration that a local Kurdish leader, Sheikh Mahmud Barzinji of Suleimaniyah, was appointed as governor in the Kurdish area of Mosul. A leader with limited legitimacy, he soon found himself in a precarious position among competing Kurdish factions. Barzinji revolted against British rule, but his rebellion was put down by brutal bombings by the Royal Air Force (RAF). The First World War had emphasised to the major powers the importance of having a secure source of petroleum, and this motivated the British to attach the area of Mosul to Iraq so that the latter may become an economically viable entity.

The next Iraqi Kurd leader to emerge was Mulla Mustafa Barzani. In 1946 he founded the Kurdish Democratic Party (KDP), which continues to play a prominent role in Kurdish politics. Barzani's son, Massoud, is now the leader of the party and the president of the KRG. The younger Barzani's role in the region has been critical to both the accommodation and censure of regional Kurdish movements dependent on personal power and patronage. He is not an undisputed leader of Kurds, however, as followers of his rival, Jalal Talabani, insist. Talabani is currently the president of Iraq and the leader of the Patriotic Union of Kurdistan (PUK). In contrast to the KDP, Talabani's party appeals to the left-leaning, urban, Kurdish elite, and its main stronghold is Suleiymaniye. Talabani draws on his good relations with the Iranian ruling and business elites to legitimise his party's dominating presence in Kurdish and Iraqi politics. His family and the PUK own one of the largest oil and construction consortia in Iraq, the Nokan group. The company facilitates, in large part, the multibillion dollar trade with Iran in the PUK's green zone and is able to influence future scenarios in the Kurdish region.

The PUK views the KDP as a conservative and tribal party that seeks unwarranted accommodation with both Turkey and Baghdad. The PUK's primary regional patron is Iran, which supported its early ideological and material establishment. Intra-Kurdish rivalry between Talabani and Barzani has led to severe internal divisions among Iraqi Kurds. In 1994, these tensions culminated in a four-year-long civil war between the two factions. In this way, the Kurds of Iraq have faced a double bind, the inability of their own movements to achieve unity, and the battle for recognition as full citizens of Iraq.

The Iraqi Kurdish experience has shown that, in addition to legal acknowledgement of their minority status, sufficient economic muscle is needed to maintain stability in the area. Thus, despite being mentioned in the first Iraqi Constitution of 1958 as a distinct minority, Kurds lacked de facto power on a local government level. The Iran-Iraq war was a pivotal moment for the Kurdish movement and its leaders, who chose to align themselves with Iran against Saddam Hussein. Predictably, Saddam's response was brutal and the Kurds were thereafter considered traitors to the nation. In 1987, a chemical warfare campaign destroyed Kurdish villages, and the Halabja massacre, during which thousands of civilians were murdered, stands out as one of Iraq's darkest hours.

With Saddam's thirst for regional expansion unquenched, the Iraqi invasion of Kuwait provided the excuse for international military intervention in Iraq, and created the opportunity for an unprecedented domestic uprising. The problem, however, was that protests began to assume sectarian undertones that, until today, dog Iraqi politics. Shi'as, who make up a sizeable proportion of the Iraqi population, began their own rebellion. This presented Baghdad with restive flanks in both the northern and the southern parts of the country, and it was not long before they too were crushed by the regime. Nevertheless, the fact that Kurds were confined to northern Iraq gave them a de facto territory upon which they could exercise power, and, following the 1991 US-imposed no-fly zone, the region was essentially demarcated as Kurdish territory. This gave way to the creation of an autonomous region that sought the trappings of a state through the holding of elections and the formation of a regional government. The territory, however, had a crucial limitation: lack of financial independence from the central authority in Baghdad.

Ironically, large parts of Iraq's oil wealth lies in what came to be Kurdish-dominated northern Iraq. Previously, the British had used the prospect of an oil-rich Kurdish area as a reason for attaching the region to its mandate territory of Iraq. The Kurds, however, seek a detachment of the region from Baghdad in order to use the wealth for their state-building venture. The most contested area remains Kirkuk and its outlying areas that, despite a fall in output over the years, are still considered to have significant capacity for oil production. Kirkuk is part of areas commonly referred to as 'Disputed Territories', and include Ninawa, Kirkuk and Diyala Governorates. According to the 2005 Iraqi Constitution, the Disputed Territories are recognised as regions that were subject to an Arabisation policy under Saddam's Ba'ath party; however, they have not been assigned to the KRG.

The central government would be loath to give up such a financially lucrative area, and is also cautious not to contribute to agitating Turkmens, Arabs and Christian Assyrians who would find themselves minorities within a Kurdish-dominated state, should the areas be given to the KRG. It has been argued that the Iraqi constitution reflects most strongly the change in power relations between the Kurdish north and the weakened central government in Baghdad. However, the constitution does not enunciate the limits of federalism, and allows the provinces to join new autonomous regions without stipulating a threshold on the number of provinces that may follow this route. This has created further contestation over the notion of 'decentralised autonomy', and begs the question of whether and to what extent this may lay the foundation for full independence. Crucially, the main supporters of this constitutional arrangement have been the Kurds and members of the Islamic Supreme Council of Iraq (ISIC), which sees itself as a representative of Iraq's Shi'a community. ISIC's main area of influence is southern Iraq, and it has been strongly influenced by the Iranian regime in its formation and ideological orientation. Nevertheless, beyond their common dislike of the authorities in Baghdad, there is little to suggest that the Kurds and the Shi'as may be able to develop a coordinated strategy to achieve their aims.

This disjuncture emphasises the misguided politicisation of ethnicity and sectarianism in Iraq, which has created the current dilemma for both Kurds and minority Shi'as alike. Their choice is either to hollow out the state by following their own trajectory (which comes at the price of instability and hostility), or to work within a unified Iraq towards the democratisation of the country as a whole. Joost Hiltermann astutely captures the quandary when he wrote, 'This politics created the fertile ground on which could be sown the seeds of federalism defined by ethnic or sectarian identity'.[3] The US strategy of a tripartite division of Iraq has undermined the ability of the state to remain a cohesive unit, and has, instead, encouraged division as a means to popularise illegal US campaigns in Iraq. 'What better way to comfort (and mobilize) people in a situation of chaos and uncertainty than to offer them protection of their nominal communities – Arabs and Kurds, Sunnis and Shiites, and sundry ethnic and confessional minorities – and their affiliated militias'.[4]

Regional forces play a critical role in Iraq and none are more important to the Kurdish question than Turkey and Iran. Both states are keen to maintain good relations with the KRG leadership as a means to block domestic Kurdish movements like the PKK and the PJAK in northern Iran. Economic and social stability in the KRG region has markedly surpassed other areas of the country. It has been described as the most prosperous region of Iraq, due, in great part, to

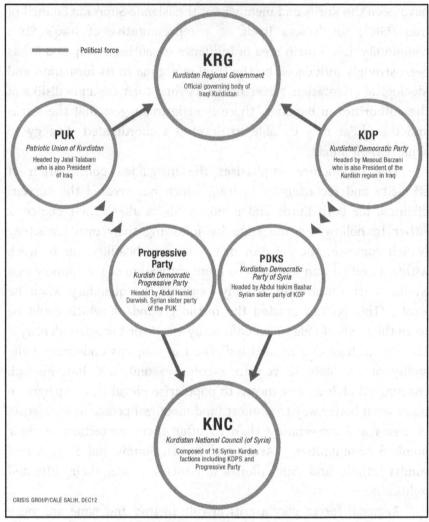

Figure 5: Parties involved in the KRG.[5]

Turkey's massive investment in its oil industry, which accounts for more than fifty per cent of foreign investment in the region. But the economic boom has not come without its challenges, as relations between Erbil and Baghdad have been further strained by the relative prosperity now enjoyed in Northern Iraq. The lack of clarity on how a 'federal' system in Iraq should actually be implemented, and, particularly, how oil revenues are to be shared, is both a technical and political issue that is a growing source of hostility between the two centres of power.

Baghdad has delayed passing the 'hydrocarbon law', which would legalise the administration of and profits from oil by the regional governments. To date, the Iraqi parliament has not moved beyond the draft bill proposed in 2007. Adnan al-Janabi, head of Iraq's parliamentary oil and energy committee explained in a recent news interview that, 'It is at the bottom of the government's list. The centralists of the ruling party have no interest to sustain a federal policy or pass a federal law...Therefore the government and IOCs (independent oil companies) will continue the risk of working in a legal vacuum.'[6]

In the absence of a formal law, the KRG has taken the risk of signing contracts with international oil companies, moves that have angered the government in Baghdad. However, the latter has also pursued multinational companies to reinvest in the country, which has predictably irritated its northern Kurdish counterpart. Baghdad is in talks with British Petroleum (BP) to rehabilitate the degraded oil wells of the Kirkuk oilfields, a region of deep-seated contestation between the Kurds and the central government. This has led to increasing distrust and disaffection between Baghdad and Erbil, bringing into question how an independent Kurdistan may survive in such a hostile climate.

There are also signs that Kurdish politicians may be overplaying their 'secessionist' card, without considering the long-term consequences of the threat. For one, a unilateral declaration of independence for Kurdistan would not be supported by major powers like the USA and the EU, who would be anxious over the regional backlash from states such as Turkey and Iran. While Turkey has sought strategic engagement with the KRG on many levels, the least of which is trade, it would not support an independent Kurdistan as this would undermine the unity project it is undertaking with its own Kurds. This is clearly demonstrated by comments by Turkey's Energy Minister, Taner Yildiz, who explained that Turkey did not differentiate between the north and the south in Iraq. Turkey would also not go against international law to achieve its ends, and will continue to regard Baghdad as the primary source of authority in Iraq. 'If Iraq is considered as a whole...there should not be any differentiation between its south, north, east, or west...If having no problems with neighbours means having no principles, we just can't do that.'[7]

By alienating the rest of the Iraqi population, particularly the Sunni Arabs, the Kurds once again run the risk of bringing the battle to their doorstep. It is clear that Iraq is a hotbed of rival nationalisms, ironically made more finite by the federal constitution's devolution of power to the regions. Neither side is willing to accommodate the concept of a unified Iraq, and this will have severe consequences for the long-term legitimacy of the struggle. What is needed is visionary leadership that can negotiate on issues based on how relevant they are to the ultimate cause of peace and security in the country. It is evident that if Iraq's leaders are influenced by greed and power, they will fail to alleviate the decades-long conflict. The Kurdish question is therefore a critical test for the long-term stability of Iraq as a whole.

Chapter Five
Paradoxical relationship with the state in Syria

Historically, Syrian Kurds have been considered foreigners in the Arab state, and their links to Turkey and northern Iraq viewed as more significant than their allegiance to Syria. In the aftermath of the collapse of the Ottoman Empire, the rise of nineteenth century Arab nationalism ensured that the ethnicisation of politics would accentuate the mistrust between various groups. Over time, centralist policies restricted the full participation of Kurds in Syrian life, leading to forcible assimilation into mainstream culture. The state, for example, outlawed the publication of materials in Kurdish languages in 1958, banned private schools from teaching in those languages, and placed significant restrictions on the ownership of property by Kurds.[1]

Ironically, however, the Alawi-dominated regime provided substantial support for the PKK and hosted its leader, Abdullah Öcalan, for more than a decade, at times reflecting a preference for Syrian Kurds over the majority Sunni population. Emphasising this double standard in policy, the Syrian administration supported the PKK's claims that it was a political organisation. During his stay in Syria, Öcalan met with high-ranking German officials and intelligence officers, with the full knowledge of the Ba'athist regime.[2] It was only in 1998, when threatened by military action from Turkey, that Damascus began to crack down on the PKK and Öcalan. Today, one-

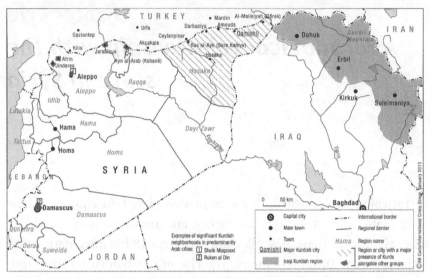

Figure 6: Majority Kurdish areas in Syria.

third of the PKK's fighting force is of Syrian-Kurdish origin.

The fissures between Syria and Turkey were deepened by a territorial dispute over Hatay province, which Turkey took control of in 1939; the strengthening of Israeli-Turkish diplomatic relations; and the 2005 launch of the South East Anatolia Project (GAP) for the sharing of water from the Euphrates River. Turkey's building of the Ataturk Dam on the Euphrates as part of the GAP project was '...perceived as Turkey's reluctance to share waters of the Euphrates with its Arab neighbours and its enthusiasm to utilize it arbitrarily'.[3] It was no surprise, then, that Syria used its leverage with the PKK as a means to influence the outcome of the water issue. Syria's approach was highlighted by Hafez al-Asad's presence at a PKK ceremony in the Bekaa Valley in Lebanon, soon after the announcement of an interruption in water flow from the Ataturk Dam.[4]

While Turkey undertook such a large-scale project in order to project its regional influence, it also desperately needed the project to demonstrate developmental goodwill in the Kurdish-dominated region where the dam was to flow through. However, the imperatives of Turkish nationalism overrode these intentions to reach out to the marginalised Kurds. The state identified a dual threat from growing Islamist movements, who demanded fair representation, as well as from the militant activities of the PKK. In the face of these 'domestic enemies', the Turkish state opted to use its comparative economic advantage to rally around a foreign enemy that would unite the country and guard the Turkey's secular structure.

This background is pertinent to understanding the evolution of Kurdish movements in Syria, and their relevance to current power dynamics at play. Heavily influenced by Syria's diplomatic relations with Turkey, Syrian Kurdish movements gained notoriety for being coopted by the regime. While Syria acquiesced to Ankara's demand that it expel Abdullah Öcalan from its territory, this did not necessarily weaken the ideological affiliation of Syrian Kurds with the PKK. In 2003, the Democratic Union Party (PYD) was created as the PKK's political branch in Syria. Indeed, many commentators have suggested that there is little to separate the PYD from the PKK. Drawing on PKK financing and experience, the PYD has established itself as the most disciplined and organised Kurdish group in Syria.

From the outset, it would have seemed that the Syrian opposition that formed since the outbreak of uprisings in 2011 had its work cut out for it. By joining up with the Kurdish armed groups who, like them, seek greater rights in Syria, and, more particularly, by forming common cause with the Kurdish PYD, the opposition could be a formidable force against the Assad regime. However, this has not been the case, because the PYD distrusts Turkey's active support for the largest opposition coalition, the National Coalition for Syrian Revolutionary and Opposition Forces, which was founded in Doha in November 2012, and the Syrian National Council (SNC), founded in Istanbul in August 2011. Ankara reversed its policy of rapprochement with Syria after unsuccessful attempts at influencing Assad to step down, and the ruling AKP party is now unabashedly opposed to the Syrian regime. Turkey is also currently hosting some 230 000 refugees registered with the UNHCR, and has spent an estimated US$600 million on Aid to Syrian refugees since the outbreak of the conflict.[5]

For Syrian Kurds, who have focused much of their energy and resources on undermining the Turkish state, Turkey's involvement raises doubts about the SNC's and the Coalition's commitment to Kurdish rights in a post-Asad scenario. The only Kurdish party from within Syria that aligned itself with the SNC was the Kurdish Future Movement Party, which was led by Mashaal Tammo until his assassination in the north-eastern city of Qamshili in October 2011. Fingers were pointed at the PYD as having collaborated with the regime to kill Tammo. The Kurdish Future Movement Party sought to establish a pluralistic Syria, as opposed to the creation of a Kurdish entity within the borders of the state. Early on in the uprisings, Bashar al Asad attempted to remove the Kurdish factor from the opposition equation by extending an offer of citizenship to thousands of Kurds in the Hasake region who had been stateless for decades.

In a telling interview, Abdul Hakim Bashar, secretary general of the Kurdish Democratic Party of Syria and chair of the Kurdish National Council (KNC), explained his party's view on the SNC. The KNC was formed in October 2011 as a Kurdish alternative to the SNC. It consists of fifteen smaller Kurdish parties, but lacks the organisational clout of the PYD. Bashar explained that Kurdish parties were being encouraged not to join the SNC.

> If the SNC fully recognizes the Kurdish Bill of Rights, we
> will join the SNC fully. Because we are very concerned
> that the SNC is so much influenced by Turkey now, they
> may postpone guaranteeing our rights until after the
> regime falls. (In the interim)...all Syrian Kurdish groups
> decided in Erbil to freeze any participation of Kurdish

> groups in the SNC. This applies to all Kurdish parties,
> from the Damascus Declaration on, and will continue
> until and unless the SNC listen to our demands.[6]

Bashar also explained that Syrian Kurds demanded self-determination within the current borders of Syria, as opposed to greater rights within a broader Syrian political environment.

Added to these fissures were allegations from other Kurdish parties that the Asad regime had capitalised on Kurdish anti-Turkish sentiment and granted the PYD calculated leeway to take over northern Syria upon the withdrawal of regime forces from the area. This arrangement would have benefitted both Asad and the PYD in the short term. For Asad, the withdrawal would allow his troops to concentrate on other areas where Syrian opposition groups had taken decisive control. Placing the PYD on the Syrian–Turkish border again projects Asad's winning card against Ankara, and raises the stakes in the Turkish domestic scenario, where a fledgling peace process is underway between the Turkish state and the PKK. The PYD/PKK's notorious intolerance of opposition would also make them the perfect guardians of the Kurdish-dominated north, ensuring that groups like the Future Movement Party, who seek to join the broader Syrian opposition, would be quashed or, at least, undermined.

In July 2012, the PYD and the KNC agreed to join forces under the leadership of Massoud Barzani, head of the Kurdish Regional Government (KRG) in Iraq. Together, they now form the major components of the Kurdish Supreme Committee, whose mission is the protection of 'liberated' Kurdish areas. Barzani brings international legitimacy that the PYD lacks, while the PYD has organisational and military astuteness that the fractured KNC coalition is sorely in need of. This marriage of convenience is, however, likely to be short lived for a number of reasons, the most important of which is the KRG's relationship with Turkey.

Barzani's increasingly close ties to Ankara are no secret. Indeed, the recent and ongoing economic boom in the KRG, which has marked it out as the most prosperous region in Iraq, is in large part due to Turkish investments and trade with the region. In exchange for stability in the KRG, Barzani has openly rejected the PKK's stance on armed activities in Turkey, thus highlighting serious ideological and political differences in their calculation of their working relationship.

As recently as January this year, a war of words broke out between the PYD and the KRG over the former's alleged use of force to assert itself on Syrian Kurds. The PYD retaliated by accusing the KRG of closing the border between northern Syria and Iraqi Kurdistan at a time when Syrian Kurds were in need of basic humanitarian supplies. Barzani's office released a statement of warning. It did not name the PYD explicitly, but was clear enough to have been directed at the organisation. It stated, in part:

> We make it clear to our brethren in West Kurdistan that we in the Kurdistan Region will not allow our border with Syria to be used for smuggling weapons and illegal drugs by any side; such misleading reports only serve the agenda of some sides... This is a critical juncture and no side should be allowed to impose itself through weapons.[7]

It is likely that a split in the upper echelons of the PKK could be a strong contributing factor in the belligerence of the PKK in Syria. The PYD's increasing boldness in Syria may be linked to the concurrent talks between the Turkish state and the PKK. Commentators have suggested that a PKK faction in Erbil may be under the influence of hardliners like the acting commander, Murat Karayilan, who is also the executive chair of the Kurdish umbrella organisation, the KCK. It has not been ruled out that a hawkish wing of the PKK, in collaboration with the PYD, may have been responsible for the killing of three PKK activists in Paris shortly after the first publicised talks with Öcalan on Imrali Island. One of the murdered activists was a close friend of Öcalan. Could it be that the Syrian conflict is being exploited to raise the stakes in the negotiations with Turkey? Or are Syrian Kurds inspired by the success of the KRG in northern Iraq and are disregarding any working relationship with non-Kurdish actors, with the support of sponsor states such as Iran? These questions are unlikely to be answered satisfactorily. What can be said is that the Kurdish question has become a critical 'swing' issue in the region. However, it is important to acknowledge the limitations of seeking to understand the conflict and its implications using the 'main actors' as a prism to reflect any change or continuity. We may ask how representative any of the groups are of the aspirations of the Kurdish people on a local level.

Calls for the creation of a state of Kurdistan have been loudest among Kurds in exile, especially the PKK, people who are, perhaps, most removed from the daily experiences of having to coexist with other groups in the region. Questions such as, 'To what extent do the interests of the political elites and the Kurdish people overlap?' and 'How influential are the goals of regional and international powers on Kurdish interests?' will be only partly addressed if we focus on dominant actors to understand the conflict.

In a thought-provoking subsection to its report on Syria's Kurds,[8] the International Crisis Group (ICG) detailed developments pertaining to some sections of Kurdish youth in Syria, who have not grabbed widespread attention. The report described anti-government protests by Kurdish youth who organised themselves according to 'local coordination committees' (LCCs) model, which included the Kurdish Youth Movement, the Union of Kurdish Youth Coordination and Kurdish Youth Union. These youth groups mobilised collective action through the use of social media. A Syrian Kurdish journalist quoted by the ICG explained that, 'These protestors [the LCCs] see themselves as part of the opposition, and when the government cracks down in Homs and Hama, the Kurdish LCCs try to show solidarity with those areas'.[9]

It seems that the LCC's activities were perceived as a threat by the traditional Kurdish parties, all of which, except for the Future Movement Party, were reluctant to join anti-regime protests. By choosing to follow the Syrian opposition lead for complete regime change, the LCCs opened themselves up to censure from entrenched Kurdish parties, especially the PYD.

The LCCs fell victim to intra-Kurdish struggles that have marred the regional movement since the rise of armed activism in 1925. However, it is clear that the lack of support given to the youth who chose unity of Syria over a secessionist Kurdish identity was a major reason for its poor showing.

Chapter Six
Hardly visible in Iran

The Kurds of Iran have had much less visibility on the international political agenda than their counterparts in the region. This may be ascribed to a greater linguistic and cultural assimilation with the dominant Persian culture, but perhaps also important has been the Iranian regime's low threshold for dissidence that has played a significant part in silencing political debate regarding the Kurds in that country. Iran has, since the Islamic Revolution in 1979, marked itself out as the guardian of Islam in the region, and, more particularly, as the champion of Shi'a Muslims around the world. Thus, Kurds have found themselves restricted by their status as both an ethnic minority with loyalties across Iran's border, and also as adherents of Sunni Islam.

Any discussion of Kurds in Iran will be insufficient if it does not consider the relationship between the post-1979 Iranian regime and the Turkish state. Rivalry between the Ottomans and Safavids was a low point in Islamic history, as each sought dominance over the ideological and geopolitical heart of the Islamic empire. The tensions between Iran and modern Turkey were less about dominating the Islamic agenda in the region, as the secular Kemalist elite in Turkey aimed to sever all ties to its Muslim past. Instead, Turkey's foreign policy before 2002 was defined by its firm relations with the USA, Europe and Israel, countries which are avowedly opposed by Iran.

The PKK, which, like Iran, opposed the nationalist regime in

Ankara, found a receptive ear in Tehran if only for its self-interested aim of destabilising Turkey. The contradictions between Iran's support for Kurds outside its borders and intolerance for Kurdish movements domestically was a key indicator of the Kurdish vulnerability to sponsor states for financial and logistical support. Until the 1990s, the main Kurdish opposition party was the Kurdistan Democratic Party of Iran (KDPI). It has, however, not taken up arms against the government, and like other Kurdish groups in the region, has historically been based in Iraq's KRG territory.

The Free life Party of Kurdistan (PJAK) is the most significant non-state armed force in Iran. PJAK is the only group that has ventured into the domestic urban environment, focusing its attacks on installations in Iran's big cities. However, due to Iran's support of Kurdish movements elsewhere, the PJAK has found itself with limited impact on the overall Iranian political landscape.

The dramatic change in Turkey's Middle East policy has also helped to curtail Iranian support for the PKK. The rapprochement between Turkey and Iran could be said to have started some ten years ago with Turkish President Ahmet Necdet Sezer's two-day visit to Iran. That was the beginning of a vigorous new era of trade and investment between the two countries, which coincided with a massive boom in the Turkish economy in general. For example, in the first quarter of 2011, Iran was the leading exporter of crude oil to Turkey, with a thirty per cent share of Turkey's total oil imports, while it was also the third largest provider of Turkey's natural gas, after Russia and Iraq.[1]

Aside from boosting the Turkish economy, Iran's diplomatic relations with Turkey have given it a powerful regional ally that has acted to neutralise negative western economic sanctions. Turkey's membership of NATO also gives Turkey the strategic ability to raise Iranian concerns regarding peace and security in the region on an international platform. The nuclear development programme is a case in point. Turkey defends Iran's right to possess nuclear capability for peaceful purposes, but has also called on the Iranian regime to open itself up to IAEA inspection. Turkey has adopted the role of mediator between the West and Iran.

In this way, the Kurds of Iran found themselves, over the past few years, squeezed by a growing economic alliance between Iran and Turkey. Iran would also not support the creation of an independent Kurdistan due to the Kurdish movement's historical relations with Israel, which has sought to use the Kurds as a destabilising force in Middle East. An Israeli-allied state on Iran's doorstep will only complicate an already volatile border situation that is developing due to Syria's complex emergency. Turkey's diplomatic victory over the Netanyahu government regarding the 2010 Mavi Marmara incident solidified Turkey's ideological engagement with its Arab neighbours, but also confirms that the Kurdish issue is intertwined with its relations with Israel. An example of Israel's increasing role in the Kurdistan region is the military support and training it has been giving to PKK commandos on Greek Cypriot territory in 2008. The fall out between Israel and Turkey as a result of the Mavi Marmara incident emboldened Israel to seek better relations with the PKK and PJAK. In 2012, Turkish Cypriot leader Dervis Eroğlu referred to this relationship, saying that some 3 000 PKK commandos were being trained by the Israeli military.[2] From the Israeli perspective, it is a strategic move to develop and nurture such a relationship with the PKK, as it would enable Israel to have a proxy force on the doorsteps of Iran and Turkey, allowing it greater access to the region for its own foreign policy objectives. A few years earlier, in 2003, Israel also developed relationships with Iraqi Kurds in an attempt to cultivate a proxy in Iraq.[3] The Israeli relationship with Iraqi Kurds actually goes back to 1958.[4]

The Syrian conflict has severely challenged relations between Iran and Turkey, with the former still staunchly supporting the

49

Syrian regime. Hizbullah, which is directly supported by Iran, has taken an active role in supporting the Asad regime militarily, a development that has caused a serious diplomatic challenge for Turkey. Turkey is an active sponsor of the opposition to Assad and has been vocal in its criticism of the Syrian regime, hosting several meetings and delegations of the Syrian opposition in Istanbul.

Sceptics have suggested that the Syrian conflict may reignite Iran's endorsement of and support for the PKK. This seemed to be the case in 2011, when it was clear that Turkey had begun changing its stance on the Asad regime. At the same time, the PKK's acting leader, Murat Karayilan, escaped from Iran, despite Turkish intelligence warning about his whereabouts on the Iranian side of the Kandil Mountains. Curiously, the PJAK declared a unilateral ceasefire with the Iranian government soon after Karayilan's escape. While the claims that Tehran disregarded Ankara's intelligence warnings were denied by officials in both countries, they nevertheless held traction with sectors of the Turkish media which were been sceptical of Iran's close ties to the AKP government. At this stage, it is difficult to predict to what extent this relationship can withstand the Syrian and PKK challenges.

Conclusion

The 'Kurdish issue' has evolved dramatically over the past thirty years, an evolution directly related to the constantly changing nature of state power in the post-colonial Middle East. The reliance on ethnicity and sectarianism as a means of monopolising state authority has been entrenched in political governance in Iran, Iraq, Turkey and Syria. For this reason, Kurdish concerns have been manipulated by elites and regimes which seek to profit, rather than resolve, the outstanding questions relating to the Kurds as citizens of the four states.

Developments in Turkey and Syria suggest counter possibilities for the future of Kurdish communities and Kurdish political roles. On the one hand, the peace process between the major Kurdish armed group, long considered a 'terrorist' organisation, and the Turkish government is showing potential for a cessation of hostilities. On the other hand, developments in Syria and Iraq raise questions of the longevity of such a cessation, as Kurdish movements in both these countries may have greater room to manoeuvre due to the serious weakening of the ruling elites in Iraq and Syria. Certainly, when discussing developments in Syria, we cannot ignore the fact that the Syrian conflict has impacted upon Turkey, financially and politically, particularly in the aftermath of a series of attacks on the border between the two countries that has claimed the lives of many innocent civilians. For Turkey, there are potentially significant domestic costs that are associated with supporting the Syrian rebels.

The first of these is a possible renewal of support for the PYD in Syria by the Assad regime as a means of derailing any credible peace process. In this scenario, the leadership contestation between Abdullah Öcalan and more militant leaders like Murat Karayilan is likely to test the limits of both the Turkish public's and leadership's resolve to continue negotiating with the PKK to resolve the Kurdish issue. Should Karayilan and other PKK hardliners prove to be stronger, this could impact on the electoral opportunities of the AKP as it heads towards both presidential and parliamentary polls. However, it will also lay bare the fractious nature of the main opposition parties who are unable to reconcile its core of nationalists opposed to peace with the PKK, with the progressives who support the process, and who remain generally sceptical of the role of democratic politics in Turkey. For the latter, the loss of the military's unilateral power has marked a definitive loss of supremacy for the old secular elite, and has caused a crisis of identity that is likely to remain unresolved for some time.

In Iraq, ongoing tension between Baghdad and Erbil is also likely to cause some disruption to the peace process, as Prime Minister Nouri al-Maliki's government will not be disposed to supporting a resolution of the Kurdish question in Turkey. Peace and increased trade between Turkey and the KRG, though unlikely to push Turkey to recognise a Kurdish state, will however play on the anxieties of the Shi'a south, wary of a rapprochement that could embolden Iraq's northern Kurds to demand more energy and oil concessions.

In Iran, the status quo remains since PJAK has refrained from making open demands on the Iranian regime. The politics of reform is now at the forefront of Iranian politics, with the election of Hassan Rouhani as president suggests the possibility of future changes to both the ailing Iranian economy and its foreign policy. The now overt involvement of Iran in direct fighting in Syria on the side of the regime suggests the possibilities of a stronger coalition between the

Iranian government and Kurdish forces which may seek to capitalise on Asad's position as an embattled leader. This could lead to a severe challenge to the seemingly straightforward peace deal in Turkey, as armed Kurdish groups in Syria could seek to directly challenge the Turkish-backed Syrian opposition, placing more strain on Turkey's already weakened (and now accepted by many as misnamed) 'zero-problems' regional policy.

The morphing of the Syrian conflict into a sectarian Sunni versus Shi'a-Alawi conflict could easily exacerbate tensions in areas where the economy and access to resources have become focal points, as has been the case in Iraq since April 2013. Were the Syrian opposition forces to be trapped in deeper ethnic and sectarian divisions and discourses, the dream of substantive change to the status of Kurds in the region will remain a distant reality. Instead, the status quo is likely to continue, with the region remaining dependent on the ethnic separation bogey as a form of threatening power to the regional regimes, rather than implementing meaningful change that may lead to inclusionary citizenship within each of the four countries in question.

The creation of a Kurdistan nation state faces numerous challenges which, aside from the obvious political problem of divisions between Kurdish groups, also include a significant geographical challenge to defining areas that are 'Kurdish' dominated. This is due to the migration of populations across the region that has made it difficult to assign or homogenise an area as 'Kurdish'. This is particularly true in the cases of Turkey and Syria. More importantly, perhaps, is the question of whether such a state would be desirable at all.

Within the current climate of competing claims to equal citizenship, the creation of a state based on religious or ethnic origin will not only be undesirable, but will likely pose a threat to the aspirations of inclusive politics in the region. There is a great need to overcome political manoeuvring that seeks to secure short-term gains at the expense of stability and substantive citizenship in the future. Despite the continued symbolic presence of a homeland for Kurds in popular Kurdish culture and even political imagination, Kurdish discourse has changed from being one of establishing a state to finding ways in which Kurds can engage with the political reality they find themselves in. The role of the Kurdish movements has become a critical factor in determining the future of the Middle East.

Notes

Introduction
1. Gunter (2004).
2. Halliday (2005: 202).

Chapter One
1. Gunter (2004).
2. Reynolds (2012).
3. Palestinian Academic Society for the Study of International Affairs. http://www.passia.org/palestine_facts/MAPS/1916-sykes-picot-agreement.html
4. Hiltermann (2008).
5. Ureutia and Villellas (2012: 7).
6. ICG (2013).

Chapter Two
1. Reynolds (2012).
2. Yegen (2011).
3. http://en.wikipedia.org/wiki/Iraqi%E2%80%93Kurdish_conflict.
4. http://www.todayszaman.com/columnist-310442-terrorism-toll-on-turkey.html.
5. Reynolds (2012: 1).
6. http://www.todayszaman.com/columnist-309751-the-secularists-who-are-disturbed-by-peace.html.
7. Reynolds (2012).
8. Keyman (2012).
9. Turam (2008: 40).
10. Reynolds (2012: 3).
11. http://www.todayszaman.com/news-309058-main-opposition-chp-deputies-visit-syrias-assad.html.

Chapter Three
1. ICG (2013).
2. Candar (2012: 19).
3. http://www.reuters.com/article/2013/03/21/us-turkey-kurds-idUSBRE92J0OF20130321.

4. Keyman (2012). http://www.e-ir.info/2012/07/25/turkeys-new-consti-tution-transformation-democratization-and-living-together/.
5. http://www.todayszaman.com/news-310436-president-says-absence-of-turkish-flag-in-diyarbakir-a-big-mistake.html.
6. http://www.todayszaman.com/columnist-310489-what-is-in-ocalans-message.html.

Chapter Four
1. Hiltermann (2008: 32).
2. Hiltermann (2008).
3. Hiltermann (2008: 35).
4. Hiltermann (2008: 35).
5. ICG (2013).
6. http://www.iraq-businessnews.com/2013/02/13/iraq-has-little-interest-in-oil-law.html.
7. http://www.hurriyetdailynews.com/turkey-is-willing-to-xist-on-whole-iraqi-soil-energy-minister.aspx.

Chapter Five
1. ICG (2013).
2. Oktav (2003).
3. Oktav (2003: 99).
4. Oktav (2003).
5. http://www.todayszaman.com/news-306446-turkey-says-syrian-refugee-spending-exceeds-600-mln.html.
6. http://www.theatlantic.com/international/archive/2012/01/syrian-kurd-leader-revolution-wont-succeed-without-minorities.html.
7. http://insightkurdistan.com/war-of-words-over-syria-border-crossing/1249/.
8. ICG (January 2013).
9. ICG (January 2013: 9).

Chapter Six
1. Habibi (2012).
2. See, for example, http://www.youtube.com/watch?v=glTN6tNzz1g.
3. Hersh (2004). See also Abdelhadi (2006).
4. Ostrovsky (1999: 102).

References

Abdelhadi, Magdi (2006). 'Israelis "train Kurdish forces"', BBC News, 20 September. http://news.bbc.co.uk/2/hi/5364982.stm.

Candar, Cengiz (2012). *'Leaving the Mountain': How may the PKK lay down Arms? Freeing the Kurdish Question from Violence.* Istanbul: TESEV Democratization Centre. http://www.tesev.org.tr.

Gunter, Michael M (2004). 'The Kurdish question in perspective', *World Affairs* 166 (4): 197–205.

Habibi, Nader (2012). *Turkey and Iran: Growing Economic Relations Despite Western Sanctions.* Crown Centre for Middle East Studies, Brandeis University, May 2012 (62).

Halliday, Fred (2005). *The Middle East in International Relations: Power, Politics and Ideology.* Cambridge: Cambridge University Press.

Hersh, Seymour (2004). 'Plan B', *The New Yorker*, 28 June. http://www.newyorker.com/archive/2004/06/28/040628fa_fact.

Hiltermann, Joost (2008). 'To protect or to project? Iraqi Kurds and their future', *Middle East Report* 247 (38). http://www.merip.org/mer/mer247/protect-or-project.

ICG (International Crisis Group) (2013). *Syria's Kurds: A Struggle within a Struggle.* ICG Middle East Report, No. 136, 22 January.

Keyman, Fuat (2012). *Turkey's New Constitution: Transformation, Democratization, and Living Together.* Istanbul Policy Centre-National Democratic Institute. http://ipc.sabanciuniv.edu/en.

Oktav, Ozden Zeynep (2003). 'Water dispute and Kurdish separatism in Turkish–Syrian relations', *The Turkish Yearbook XXXIV*: 91–117.

Ostrovsky, Victor (1999). 'Capture of Kurdish Rebel Leader Ocalan Recalls Mossad Collaboration With Both Turkey, Kurds', *Washington Report on Middle East Affairs*, April/May: 60, 102.

Reynolds, Michael A (2012). *Echoes of Empire: Turkey's Crisis of Kemalism and the Search for an Alternative Foreign Policy.* Saban Center Analysis Paper Series Number 26 of 29. Washington, DC: The Saban Centre for Middle East Policy, Brookings Institute.

Turam, Berna (2008). 'Between Islamists and Kemalists'. *International Institute for the Study of Islam in the Modern World (ISIM) Review* 21, Spring: 40-41.

Ureutia, Pamela and Ana Villellas (2012). *Reopening the Kurdish Question: States, Communities and Proxies in a Time of Turmoil.* NOREF Report. Oslo: Norwegian Peacebuilding Resource Centre. September 2012.

Yegen, Mesut (2011). 'Facing the Kurdish issue', in Marlies Casier and Joost Jongerden (eds), *Nationalisms and Politics in Turkey: Political Islam, Kemalism and the Kurdish Issue.* New York: Routledge.

Printed in the United States
By Bookmasters